The Dreams Of A Mountain Girl

Collection of poems

Archana Subba(Biju)

BookLeaf Publishing

India | USA | UK

Dedication

Dedicated to my Baba & Aama

Preface

Dreams of a Mountain Girl is not just a collection of poems; it is a journey—both inward and outward. This book marks a new chapter in my creative exploration, a step further into the landscapes of imagination, memory, and emotion.

Through these verses, I sought to capture the whispers of a life shaped by towering peaks, winding trails, and the vast skies above. Each poem carries with it a fragment of the dreams, struggles, and quiet triumphs of a mountain girl—her yearning for the unknown, her reverence for the untamed, and her unbroken bond with the world around her.

Nature serves as the muse for much of what unfolds in these pages. The rustling of leaves, the glistening snowfields, and the steadfast mountains—these elements are not just settings; they are characters, playing their part in the tapestry of dreams.

This collection is deeply personal, yet I believe it resonates universally. Whether you have stood atop a mountain or simply dreamt of one, I hope these words evoke a sense of wonder, courage, and connection. May

they inspire you to dream a little bigger and embrace the
journeys that call out to your heart.

I am grateful to you, dear reader, for embarking on this
poetic ascent with me. With every page you turn, may
you find echoes of your own dreams amidst the verses of
a mountain girl.

Acknowledgements

This book, *Dreams of a Mountain Girl*, would not have been possible without the inspiration, guidance, and support of many remarkable individuals who have touched my life along the way.

To my family, who have been my constant refuge and strength—thank you for your unconditional love, understanding, and belief in my dreams. Your faith in me has been the bedrock of all my creative endeavors.

I extend heartfelt gratitude to the towering mountains and the serene landscapes that stirred my soul and lent their voices to my verses. Nature itself has been my greatest mentor, teaching me the language of resilience, wonder, and dreams.

To my friends and confidants, who have lent their ears and hearts to my musings—your encouragement and honest feedback have made this journey not just enjoyable but deeply fulfilling.

Finally, to the unsung moments of solitude and self-discovery that shape each of us—I am grateful for the lessons they brought, and for the poetry they inspired.

This collection is a labor of love, and it belongs as much
to all of you as it does to me. Thank you for being a part
of this journey.

1. People these days......

Their faces lit by screens, connections turned to ghosts,
While life's harsh truths unravel, neglected and
engrossed.
We scroll through fleeting moments, a world reduced to
likes,
Yet silence grows louder, drowning out the cries.

A child weeps in shadows, dreams buried in despair,
As laughter fills the void where empathy should care.
People these days young and old,
Chasing fleeting glimpses, lost stories left untold.

Instead of reaching out, they watch from far away,
Each tragedy a hashtag, just another sad cliché.
People these days young and old...
What price do we pay for the warmth we've sold?

2. Alimony - a new trend

Marriages are made in heaven
The two hearts are binded with love and promises
To be together in both worse and rosy paths

We made the rule to help the helpless
To uplift those single mothers who thrive hard to meet
ends while upbringing their children on their own.
But there are women who extorted those innocent men
who got trapped in the name of wedding vows.

Lesson to be learnt to so called feminism..
Let's not redefine it in such a way that women have to be
ashamed of.
But let's walk together to grow towards prosperity and
happiness
Keeping aside each other's ego.

3. The Mountain Calling

My eyes search for the clear blue sky.
The feel of chilling breeze rub my nose making it numb.
The smell of the soil when it mingles with the downpour
of monsoon drizzle;
Lovingly touches the flora and fauna
On the silent valley and spurs.
The natural spring flowing through the bamboo funnels
quench my thirst on a sunny summer
The dry and cold wind in the winters
Makes my skin go wrinkled and red.
The valley blooms with oranges and peaches.
Rhododendron and Orchids full the path
Like ornaments on a queen's face.
The smell of the green tea takes me back to the "teen"
me.
The pine forest and narrow creeks that surrounds the
valley
This makes it a Heaven of Hills.

4. An Ode of a Princess

Hello my Prince!
Didn't you notice my new lavender dress
It has hues of love and the fragrance of freshness in the
air.
I have a matching hat to suit my lovely dress.
Oh! My prince, haven't you noticed it yet.
My little wallet looks perfectly tucked in my palms.
No one knows it has a secret message though.
Hello! My prince..
I have been waiting for you so long ...
Don't you know?

5. A Child in Her

The wide smile on her face forms an arch with her eyes.
The warm "hello" in the morning brightens the buzzing
day.
The chit chat in between the busy hour
Releases the stress away
Fortunately she becomes an angel in disguise
Who fills one's life with good vibes.

6. My Little Black Dress

My little black dress ....

I wore this dress not to please you but to vent my

emotions

I wore it so someone would praise me and say I'm

gorgeous.....

Just for a sake though.

This off shoulder was never my choice;

But let it be so which makes me bright.

Those high heels would make me look confident

Even though I'm broken to pieces within....

7. I am far beyond the Race

I am far beyond the race my Darlings!
Don't you test my patience.
I have been tested in the burning furnace a thousand
times.
Don't you see the glow on my visage?
It's a stone that changed into a diamond
Which outshines all the crystals around.
The route I take is my choice.
Don't you dig into it as you would never have the
courage to walk on the path I have chosen.
It is wild, it is a challenge,
It is sweet and lemony at times.
Don't you dare to judge my morale...
It is far beyond your race....

8. The Womanhood

When you have a heart that feels a deep pinch within..
Wer eyes forgetting to roll down their cheeks.
Words that play to and from from heart to mind..
But still you carry a wide smile to show to the world....
That all is perfectly well
This is grace..
This is attitude..
This is integrity..
This is me and you out there.
A woman with gratitude.

9. Once lived a true Gentleman

You may be in the moon by now
Or the brightest star shining in the zade black dark
Or may be in a mother's womb growing with all rainbow
dreams.
You broke the hearts of many queens
But the whole world loves you so dear,
As you care for them so much;
Your humble gestures always melt our hearts.
How gentle you!
Who won the whole world with his love
And good deeds to one and all.

10. Frenemy

Veiled face
Concealed smile
Disguised affection
Camouflaged bonding

A search for life
A riddle to solve
A zigzag route
With multiple clues

Urgent for truth
An ounce of faith
Life is a bread
With trillions taste

11. Dream in a slumber

She comes to meet me with teary eyes
Asks for help and takes me to see her kith and kins.
The morning I wake up thinking ..
What a vivid dream it was?
Is it real or just a dream..

My mother comes and talks to me
As if we have never parted ways from this life to the
world beyond
It feels I am connecting to the people l love
Who have already left from this world within

We will meet one day I feel
Let's keep meeting in dream
Until I see the world beyond.

12. They say I'm Loud

The soul who longs to hear the river flowing by..
Who miss the humming of bees and cricket flies..
Who quench her thirst from a natural spring
Oozing out from the mountain near by.
How can you say she is loud that unease your party
lights.
The malls are lovely but have you tried a brisk walk in
the breezy daylight
The crowd of humans make you feel safe
But have you been in search of true happiness on those
lonely nights??

13. Corporate jargon

You talk about synergy
But did anyone bother when she was not able to cope
with her work from the ICU bed.

You talk about bandwidth
But did you give her an opportunity when she said she
can take up the responsibility.

She puts her best foot forward to achieve those low
hanging fruits.
Didn't you try to push it back as if it has nothing to do
with you.

Let's touch base and move the needle to deep dive with
your blue sky thinking.
Let's talk about the pain point and come together with a
win-win solution for all the drama they play to survive.

14. A wish on a moonlit night

The crescent moon shining like a diamond dangler on
the night sky
Tiny star perfectly seated on its side
How beautiful the moon is..
Like a "Mang Tika" on a bridal face

Let's make a wish ,my heart said
The moment I saw them in the night sky.

The wish I made may never come true.
But my heart is filled with love and hope,
The moment I see the brightest star perfectly
accompanying the gorgeous moon.

15. Excerpts

"Time is the biggest factor
You feel the pace when it's gone."

" Don't judge me with your might
I will flow like a river .
Don't search me in the crowd
I will vanish like a spark."

" Shuffling between the heart and the head
Don't know who is right.
Is my heart heavy or the head is overwhelming."

"Three things that I miss...
Mother's warm hug
Selfless love
Unselfish happiness."

16. Sometimes.......

Sometimes the night steals the sleep from your eyes
Making you more alive in the darkest cloud.
You feel the deepest pain and the heart feels like it
stopped beating.

Sometimes the night steals the smile from your face
And takes you back to your lonely self
Searching for your own shadow...

Sometimes......

17. Morning Bliss

The cold breeze touches my face making it numb,
As I walk down the road mesmerized by the beauty of
Bougainville and China Rose.
The green valleys are filled with tea bushes and pine
trees in between.
The Sun wakes up slowly out from the gloomy sky.
I hear the chirping of sparrows and cuckoos;
Dos on ten street silently enjoying the beauty of
morning mist.
The ladies carrying baskets on their back,
Heading towards the tea garden,
A new day for them with wide smile on their faces, so
fresh as the morning itself.
As I walk down the road, few memories so afresh
I am happy and content with the bliss around.

18. Flickering Faith

Faith in an idol
Faith in a God
Faith lies within in a human's heart.

Faith in God fills one's heart with love and care
God is unknown yet knows all well.

Blind faith covers the heart and mind.
Makes one blind and enters crime.
Hurts the loved one and all around.
Blind faith is after all blind and deranged.

19. Alas..that night

The silent Breeze at the shore swiftly dancing on the sea.
The twilight of the crescent moon flashing on the beds of
water.
Teb stars above shine so well in the dark blanket of
dawn.
So gracefully the waves dance to their own tune.
The shaft moves higher and thither in search of a prey
with a blue light on its forehead.
Solitude howls with pain
Eyes search for the open sky
Heart feels a sudden pinch within
"Life" why does this darkness comes along with the
twilight?

20. A fond Good Bye

Do not come to me to shower your love
When I am peacefully sleeping in my coffin.
Do not cover me with those beautiful fresh flowers.
Let them bloom and wither in their own space.
Do not shed tears on my corpse
As I don't like to be a reason for hurting you.
Just sit beside me and sing a soulful song.

21. An innocent mom

A teen mother says to her two little sons...
Be mischeavous but don't get caught.
How innocent a teen mother she was,
With angelic looks and innocent gesture.

Her blue eyes are so curious and blase'
Her silent yet soft words captivated the people always

Compassionate heart won the world all over.
Either young or old, they were fanatics of her.

22. Railway station to Kovalam

With milestones of dreams in my eyes.
Bouncing ball of excitement within me.
Reached by a train journey from the Queen of Hills to
God's own country.
The day with slight drizzle
Road was wet and clean.
Calm and cool weather welcomed us with greenery
within.
Headed towards the silent road
With trees besides with blooming "Kanikonna".
How beautiful it looks, the Golden Shower
Hanging all over through the straight route
As if it's welcoming us with yellow flowers.
Fell in love with the beauty of nature the day I stepped
out of the train to see the place around.
Truly it is God's own country.
How beautiful is the view of the sea
When the gorgeous sun sets over the horizon.

The crimson light flashes all over the clear sky
And the sea glitters with its shine.
23

23. Sleeping Beauty

The lilac satin gown perfectly fits on her leaner skin
How beautifully her golden hair glows like the sea waves
in the moon lit night.
Those blues eyes are almost closed
As she falls asleep on her swinging chair.
The innocence is crystal clear
The way she falls asleep like a baby dear.

24. Twilight

The Sun sets by the horizon
But I feel the pain within
Though it's crimson light promises a brighter day ahead..
Still this heart searches for a much longer twilight.
The whirlwind on the sea alarms the busy bees.
The whistles on the nearby place.
Frightened the moony night.
Thunder howls the night sky
The silver lining lights the darkest sphere.

25. Nagar Sangh Kirtan

The chanting of "Suprabhatam"
Wakes me up on the misty morning.
All come together for a "Nagar Sangh Kirtan"
With "dhol" and candles on each side
Hurrily I wake to join the sway
How lovely it feels to sing out loud.
The silence broken with the rhythm of songs
Praising the lord who is one and all.

26. Magic Wand

Take me to the place where the clock ticks
Only with my hand
Flower blooms in every doors
Where people smile with a genuine heart.
Yearn for the breeze that chill my cheeks.
Makes me feel so serene and clean.

The Sun that rise with hazy lights
The rain that drops makes the path so white.
The mountains high out there...with snowy veil.
The rivers nearby with rhododendrons and wild orchids
around.

27. A Princess's Funeral

Let me lie down now.
No drama, no love,
No pain, no hurts.
Let me lie down now
For all in vain.

Surreal it was my life with you...
Oh! My Darling Prince.
Love is what I asked for..
But it's ok now not to be a part of you though.

Let me lie down now
No drama, no love
No pain, no hurts.
Let me lie down now
For all in vain.

www.ingramcontent.com/pod-product-compliance
Lightning Source LLC
LaVergne TN
LVHW010943200726
843509LV00013B/2275